BRANCHES
OF
SCIENCE
FROM A – Z

Roy Basa

**COPYRIGHT © 2022 BRANCHES OF SCIENCE FROM
A – Z
By Roy Basa**

Edited by Marie Ezekiel
Graphic Artist and Cover Designer: Tess Ritumalta

ISBN:
Hardbound-978-621-470-318-0
MOBI/KINDLE-978-621-470-319-7
Softbound/Paperback-978-621-470-320-3

Published in the Philippines by:
**Poetry Planet Book Publishing House
Rosario, Pozorrubio, Pangasinan, Philippines
Contact No.: 09554960044**
Email: maritesritumalta@gmail.com

DEDICATION

This book is ultimately dedicated to my wife Rozel Jaena Basa, and to our children, Niel Michael, Jasper Miguel, and Amara Celestine.

Secondly, to all my students who are requesting me to write a list of all the branches of science, this is now my chance of granting your humble request. May you find this book simple yet exciting to read.

PREFACE

The Branches of Science from A to Z is specially crafted and written to respond to the needs and interests of the aspiring and inspiring students of science.

It is the ultimate goal of this book to really make the definition of 650+ branches of science as simple as possible for everybody to easily remember, learn and enjoy at the same time.

TABLE OF CONTENTS

Acanthochronology	science of cactus spines grown in a time-ordered sequence
Acarology	science of mites and ticks
Aceology	science of remedies
Acology	science of medical Remedies
Acoustics	science of sound
Actinobiology	science of ionizing radiation's effect on living matter
Adenology	science of glands
Aedoeology	science of generative Organs
Aerobiology	science of airborne Organisms
Aerodonetics	science of gliding
Aerodynamics	science of the dynamics or movement of gas
Aerolithology	science of meteorites

Aeropalynology	science of pollens and spores in the atmosphere
Aerology	science of atmosphere
Aeronautics	science of navigation through air or space
Aerophilately	science of collecting airmail stamps
Aerostatics	science of air pressure
Agnoiology	science of ignorance
Agonistics	science of art and theory of prizefighting
Agriology	science of comparing primitive peoples
Agrobiology	science of plant nutrition and soil yields
Agroecology	science of the application of ecological processes to agriculture
Agrogeology	science of agrominerals
Agrology	science of agricultural soils

Agronomics	science of land Productivity
Agrostology	science of grasses
Alethiology	science of truth
Algedonics	science of pain and Pleasure
Algology (botany)	science of algae
Algology (Medicine)	science of pain
Anesthesiology	science of anesthetics
Anaglyptics	science of carving in low Relief
Anagraphy	science of constructing Catalogues
Anatomy	science of the structure of the body
Andragody	science of adult Education
Andrology	science of men's Physique

Anemology	science of wind
Angiology	science of blood flow and lymphatic system
Anthropobiology	science of human biology
Anthropology	science of human culture
Anthrozoology	science of human – animal Interaction
Apiology	science of bees
Aquatic ecology	science of the aquatic Environment
Aphnology	science of wealth
Arachnology	science of spiders
Archaeology	science of human remains
Archelogy	science of first principles
Archology	science of the origin of Government
Arctophily	science of teddy bears
Areology	science of Mars

Aretaics	science of virtue
Aristology	science of dining
Arthrology	science of joints
Arthropodology	science of arthropods
Astacology	science of crayfish
Asteroseismology	science of star Oscillations
Astheniology	science of weakening and Aging
Astrobiology	science of extraterrestrial Life
Astrobotany	science of plants in space
Astrodynamics	science of the motion of rockets and spacecraft
Astrogeology	science of extraterrestrial Geology
Astrometeorology	science of the effect of stars on climate
Astronomy	science of celestial bodies

Astrophysics	science of the behavior of interstellar matter
Astroseismology	science of star oscillations
Atmology	science of aqueous vapor
Audiology	science of hearing
Autecology	science of ecology of one Species
Autology	science of oneself
Auxology	science of growth
Avionics	science of electronic devices for aircraft
Axiology	science of the ultimate nature of value

Bacteriology	science of bacteria
Balneology	science of the therapeutic benefit of bath
Barodynamics	science of bridges
Barology	science of gravitation
Bathymetry	science of underwater Depth
Batology	science of brambles
Bibliology	science of books
Bibliotics	science of document's Authenticity
Bioecology	science of the interaction of life in the environment
Biogeochemistry	science of the surface of the earth
Biology	science of life
Biochemistry	science of chemical processes and their relationship to the organism

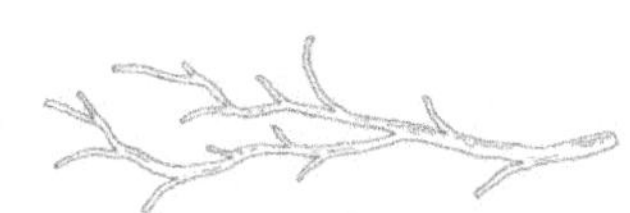

Biomechanics	science of structure, functions, and motion of the biological system
Biometrics	science of biological Measurement
Biophysics	science of biological phenomena in relation to physics
Biopsychology	science of applying biology to studying man's behavior
Biotribology	science of friction, wear, and lubrication of the biological system
Bionomics	science of organisms interacting in their environments
Botany	science of plants
Bromatology	science of food
Brontology	science of thunder
Bryology	science of mosses and liverworts

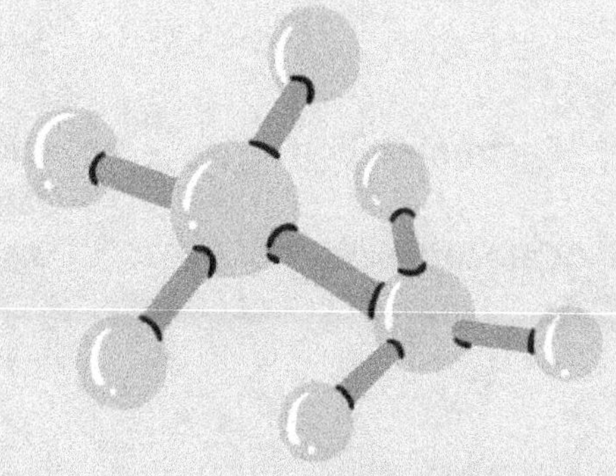

Cacogenics	science of racial Degeneration
Caliology	science of bird's nests
Calorifics	science of heat
Cambistry	science of international Exchange
Campanology	science of bells
Carcinology	science of crabs and Crustaceans
Cardiology	science of hearts
Caricology	science of sedges
Carpology	science of fruit
Cartography	science of making maps and globes
Cartophily	science of collecting cigarette cards
Castrametation	science of designing a camp
Catacoustics	science of echoes

Catallactics	science of commercial Exchange
Catechetics	science of teaching by questions and answer
Cell biology	science of prokaryotic and eukaryotic cells
Cetology	science of whales and Dolphins
Chalcography	science of engraving copper and brass
Chalcotriptics	science of taking rubbings from ornamental brasses
Chaology	science of chaos theory
Characterology	science of character
Chemistry	science of matter
Chirocosmetics	science of manicure
Chirography	science of penmanship
Chirology	science of hands
Chiropody	science of feet

Chorology	science of the geographic description of anything
Chrematistics	science of wealth and political economy
Chronobiology	science of biological Rhythms
Chrysology	science of precious Metals
Ciselure	science of chasing metals
Climatology	science of climate
Clinology	science of aging
Codicology	science of manuscripts
Coleopterology	science of beetles and Weevils
Cometology	science of comets
Conchology	science of shells
Coprology	science of pornography
Cosmetology	science of cosmetics

Cosmology	science of celestial Bodies
Craniology	science of the skull
Criminology	science of crime
Cryobiology	science of life under cold Conditions
Cryptology	science of codes
Cryptozoology	science of animals whose existence has no conclusive proof
Ctetology	science of inheritance of acquired characteristics
Cynology	science of dogs
Cytology	science of cells

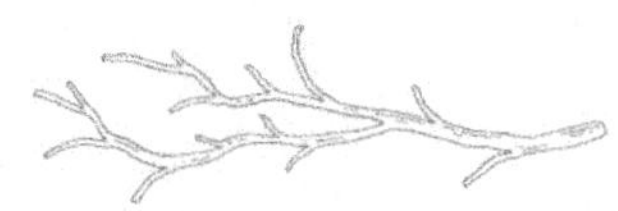

Dactyliology	science of rings
Dactylography	science of fingerprints
Dactylogy	science of sign language
Deltiology	science of collecting post – cards
Demography	science of populations
Demology	science of human population, behavior, and activities
Demonology	science of demons
Dendrochronology	science of tree rings
Dendrology	science of trees
Deontology	science of moral Obligation
Dermatoglyphics	science of skin patterns and fingerprinting
Dermatology	science of skin
Desmology	science of ligaments

Diabology	science of devils
Diagraphics	science of making diagrams and drawings
Dialectology	science of dialects
Dioptrics	science of light refraction
Diplomatics	science of deciphering ancient writings and texts
Diplomatology	science of diplomats
Docimology	science of assaying
Dosiology	science of doses
Dramaturgy	science of producing and staging dramatic works
Dysgenics	science of racial Degeneration
Dysteleology	science of vestigial Organs

Ecclesiology	science of church affairs
Eccrinology	science of excretion
Ecology	science of environment
Economics	science of material Wealth
Edaphology	science of soils
Egyptology	science of ancient Egypt
Ekistics	science of human Settlement
Electrochemistry	science of the relationship between electricity and chemicals
Electrology	science of electricity
Electrostatics	science of static electricity
Embryology	science of embryos
Emetology	science of vomiting
Emmenology	science of menstruation
Endemiology	science of local disease

Endocrinology	science of glands
Enigmatology	science of enigmas
Entomology	science of insects
Entozoology	science of parasites
Enzymology	science of enzymes
Ephebiatrics	science of medicine dealing with adolescence
Epidemiology	science of epidemics
Epileptology	science of epilepsy
Epistemology	science of grounds of Knowledge
Eremology	science of deserts
Ergology	science of effects of work on human
Ergonomics	science of people at work
Escapology	science of freeing oneself from constraints

Eschatology	science of death and final Matters
Ethnogeny	science of origins of races
Ethnology	science of cultures
Ethnomethodology	science of everyday Communication
Ethnomusicology	science of comparative musical systems
Ethnology	science of natural Character
Ethonomics	science of economic and ethical principles of society
Etiology	science of causes
Etymology	science of the origin of Words
Euthenics	science of improving living conditions
Exobiology	science of extraterrestrial life

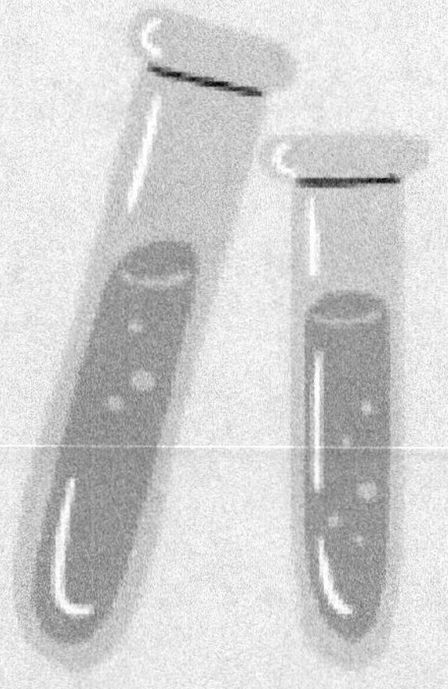

Felinology	science of felines
Finance	science of managing money
Floristry	science of cultivating Flowers
Fluid dynamics	science of the flow of Fluids
Fluid mechanics	science of the behavior of fluid at rest and in motion
Fluid statics	science of the behavior of fluids at rest
Fluviology	science of watercourses
Folkloristics	science of folklores and Fables
Forestry	science of managing forests and related resources
Fracture Mechanics	science of propagation of cracks in materials
Futurology	science of future

Garbology	science of garbage
Gastroenterology	science of the digestive System
Gastronomy	science of fine dining
Gemmology	science of gems and Jewels
Gender studies	science of gender
Genealogy	science of descent of families
Genesiology	science of reproduction and heredity
Genetics	science of heredity and Variations
Geochemistry	science of earth's crust
Geochronology	science of measuring geologic time
Geography	science of the surface of the earth and its inhabitants
Geology	science of earth
Geometry	science of sizes, shapes, positions, angles, and dimensions of things
Geomorphogeny	science characteristics, origins, and development of landforms

Geomorphology	science of landforms and landform evolution
Geoponics	science of agriculture
Geotechnics	science of increasing habitability of the earth
Geratology	science of decadence and Decay
Gerocomy	science of old age
Gerontology	science of the elderly and Aging
Gigantology	science of giants
Glaciology	science of ice ages and Glaciation
Glossology	science of language
Glyptology	science of gem engraving
Gnomonics	science of measuring time using sundials
Gnoseology	science of knowledge; philosophy of knowledge
Gnotobiology	science of life in germ–free Conditions
Graminology	science of grasses
Grammatology	science of the systems of writing

Graphology	science of handwriting
Gromatics	science of surveying
Gynaecology	science of women's Physiology
Gyrostatics	science of rotating bodies

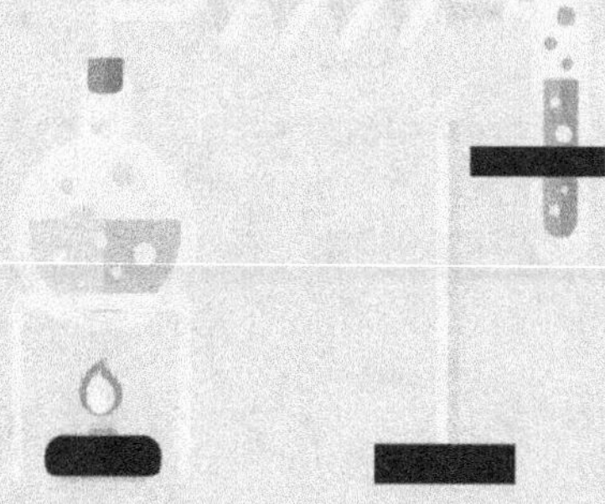

Haemataulics	science of movement of blood through blood vessels
Hagiology	science of saints
Halieutics	science of fishing
Hamartiology	science of sin
Harmonics	science of musical acoustics
Hedonics	science of ethics or things that deals with pleasure
Helcology	science of ulcers
Heliology	science of the sun
Helioseismology	science of the sun's interior
Helminthology	science of worms
Hematology	science of blood
Hemodynamics	science of the dynamics of blood circulation
Hepatology	science of liver, gall bladder, and pancreas
Heredity	science of transmission of traits from parents to offspring
Heresiology	science of heresies
Hermeology	science of Mercury

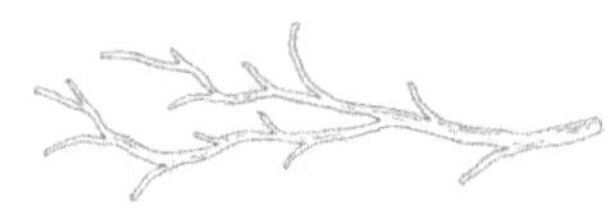

Herpetology	science of reptiles and Amphibians
Hierology	science of sacred matters
Hippiatrics	science of diseases of Horses
Hippology	science of horses
Histology	science of body tissues
Histopathology	science of diseases of body tissues
Historiography	science of history writing
Historiology	study of history
Homiletics	science of preaching
Home Economics	science of the relationship between home and economics
Hoplology	science of the human combative behavior and performance
Horography	science of constructing Sundials
Horology	science of time Measurement
Horticulture	science of gardening

Hydrobiology	science of aquatic Organisms
Hydrodynamics	science of the movement of liquids
Hydrogeology	science of groundwater
Hydrography	science on investigating bodies of water
Hydrokinetics	science of the motion of Liquids
Hydrology	science of water resources
Hydrometeorology	science of atmospheric Moisture
Hydropathy	science of treating diseases with water
Hydrostatics	science of fluids behavior at rest
Hyetology	science of rainfall
Hygiastics	science of health and Hygiene
Hygienics	science of sanitation
Hygiology	science of cleanliness
Hygroscopy	science of humidity
Hygrometry	science of humidity

Hymnography	science of writing hymns
Hymnology	science of hymns
Hypnology	science of sleep and Hypnosis
Hypsography	science of measuring heights

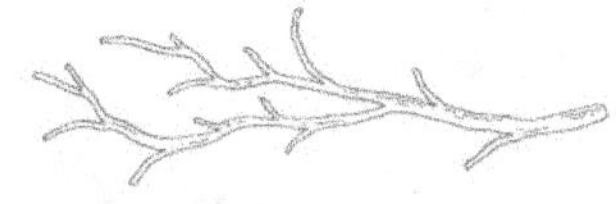

Iamatology   science of remedies

Iatrology   science of treatise on
                             medical topics; study of
                             medicine

Iatromathematics   science of archaic practice
                             of medicine in relation to
                             astrology

Ichnography   science of drawing
                             Plans

Ichnology   science of fossilized footprints

Ichthyology   science of fish

Iconography   science of drawing symbols

Iconology   science of icons

Ideogeny   science of the origins of
                             Ideas

Ideology   science of ideas used to
                             explain behavior

Idiomology   science of idiom; jargon or
                             Dialect

Idiopsychology   science of one's own mind

Immunochemistry   science of immune system

Immunogenetics   science of genetic
                             characteristics of immunity

Immunology   science of immunity

Immunopathology science of immunity to Disease

Insectology science of insects

Irenology science of peace

Iridology science of iris of the eye

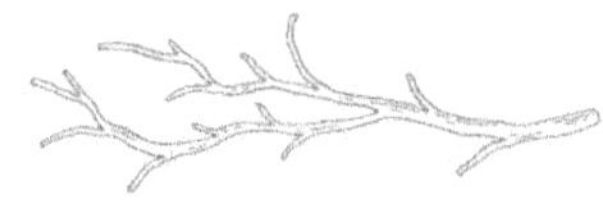

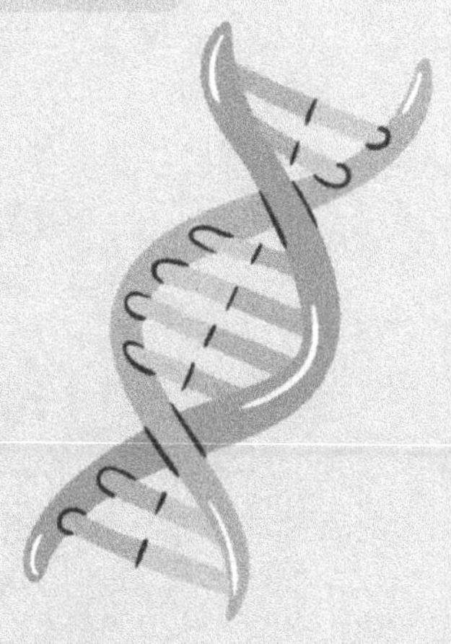

Kalology	science of beauty
Karyology	science of cell nuclei
Kinematics	science of motion
Kinesics	science of gestural Communication
Kinesiology	science of human movement and posture
Kinetics	science of forces producing or changing motion
Koniology	science of atmospheric pollutants and dust
Ktenology	science of putting people to death
Kymatology	science of wave motion

Labeorphily	science of collecting and studying beer bottle labels
Larithmics	science of population Statistics
Laryngology	science of larynx
Lepidopterology	science of butterflies and Moths
Leprology	science of leprosy
Lexicology	science of words and their Meanings
Lexigraphy	science of defining words
Lichenology	science of lichens
Limacology	science of slugs
Limnobiology	science of freshwater Ecosystems
Limnology	science of bodies of fresh Water
Linguistics	science of language
Liturgiology	science of liturgical forms and church rituals
Loimology	science of plagues and Epidemics

Loxodromy	science of sailing along rhumb – lines
Ludology	science of games

Macroeconomics   science of dealing with the large scale or whole economy

Magirics   science of cookery

Magnanerie   science of raising silkworms

Magnetics   science of magnetism

Magnetohydrodynamics   science of electrically conducting fluids

Magnetostatics   science magnetic fields in steady motion

Malacology   science of mollusks

Malariology   science of malaria

Mammalogy/Mastology   science of mammals

Manege   science of horsemanship

Mariology   science of studying the Virgin Mary

Marine biology   science of ocean ecosystem

Mathematics   science of magnitude, numbers, and forms

Mazology   science of mammals

Mechanics   science of the action of force on bodies

Meconology	science of treatise concerning opium
Media Studies	science of mass media
Medicine	science of diagnosing, treating, and preventing disease
Melissopalynology	science of honey
Melittology	science of bees
Melology	science of music
Mereology	science of part-whole Relationships
Metallogeny	science of the origin and distribution of metal deposits
Metallography	science of the structure and constitution of metals
Metallurgy	science of alloying and treating metals
Metaphysics	science of studying the principles of nature and thought
Metapolitics	science of politics in theory or abstract
Metapsychology	science of nature of the Mind

Metascience	science of studying science
Meteoritics	science of meteors
Meteorology	science of weather
Methodology	science of studying the description of methods
Methyology	science of alcohol
Metrics	science of versification
Metrology	science of weights and Measures
Microanatomy	science of microscopic Tissues
Microbial ecology	science of the microbial Environment
Microbiology	science of microscopic Organisms
Microclimatology	science of local climates
Microeconomics	science of dealing small scale or local economy
Micrology	science of discussing Trivialities
Micropaleontology	science of microscopic Fossil
Microphytology	science of very small plant life

Microscopy	science of studying minute objects; a microscope
Mineralogy	science of minerals
Molecular biology	science of molecular basis of biological activity in and between cells
Molinology	science of mills and milling
Momilogy	science of mummies
Morphology	science of forms and the development of structures
Muscology	science of mosses
Museology	science of museums
Musicology	science of music
Mycology	science of fungi
Myology	science of muscles
Myrmecology	science of ants
Mythology	science of myths; fables and tales

Naology	science of church or temple architecture
Nosology	science of the nose
Nautics	science of navigation
Necroplanetology	science of the destruction of planets
Nematology	science of nematodes
Neonatology	science of newborn babies
Neossology	science nestling birds
Nephology	science of clouds
Nephrology	science of kidneys
Neurobiology	science of the nervous System
Neuroeconomics	science of human decision-making to process alternatives
Neurology	science of the nervous system
Neuropsychology	science of studying the relationship between the brain and behavior
Neurypnology	science of hypnotism

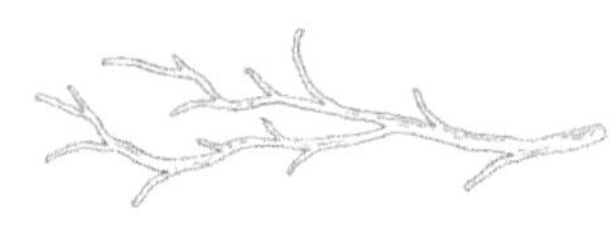

Netrosophy	science of the origin and nature of philosophical neutralities
Nomology	science of laws; especially of the mind
Noology	science of the intellect
Nosology	science of diseases
Nostology	science of senility
Notaphily	science of collecting bank – notes, and cheques
Numerology	science of studying numbers in pseudoscientific way
Numismatics	science of coins
Nymphology	science of nymphs
Nanotechnology	science of nanite

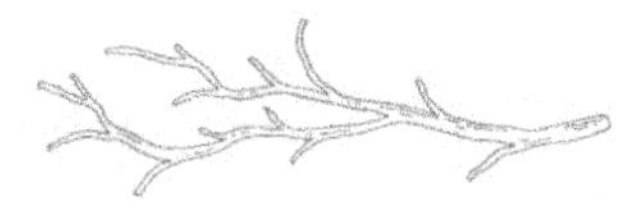

Obstetrics	science of midwifery
Oceanography	science of oceans
Oceanology	science of oceans
Odontology	science of teeth
Odonatology	science dragonflies and damselflies
Oenalogy	science of wines
Oikology	science of housekeeping
Olfactology	science of the sense of smell
Ombrology	science of rain
Oncology	science of tumors
Oneirology	science of dreams
Onomasiology	science of nomenclature
Onomastics	science of proper names
Ontology	science of pure being; nature of things
Oology	science of eggs
Ophiology	science of snakes
Ophthalmology	science of eye diseases
Optics	science of light

Optology	science of sight
Optometry	science of examining the Eye
Orchidology	science of orchids
Ornithology	science of birds
Orology	science of mountains
Orthoepy	science of correct Pronunciation
Orthography	science of spelling
Orthopterology	science of cockroaches
Oryctology	science of minerals
Osmics	science of smell
Osmology	science of smell and olfactory processes
Osphresiology	science of smell
Osteology	science of bones
Otology	science of the ear
Otorhinolaryngology	science of ear, nose, and throat

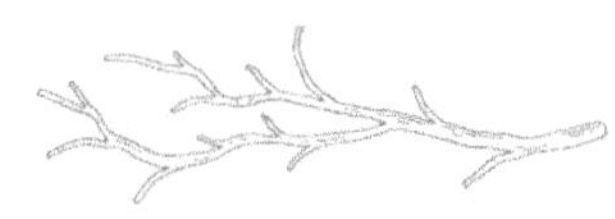

Paedology	science of children
Paidonosology	science of children's diseases; pediatrics
Paleoanthropology	science of early humans
Paleobiology	science of fossil plants and animals
Paleoclimatology	science of ancient climates
Paleoichthyology	science of ancient fish
Paleolimnology	science of ancient lakes
Paleontology	science of fossils
Paleopedology	science of early soils
Paleobotany	science of ancient plants
Paleoosteology	science of ancient bones
Palynology	science of pollen
Papyrology	science of paper
Paradoxology	science of paradoxes
Parapsychology	science of unexplained mental phenomena
Parasitology	science of parasites
Paroemiology	science of proverbs
Parthenology	science of virgins

Pataphysics	science of imaginary solutions
Pathology	science of disease
Patrology	science of studying early Christianity
Pedagogics	science of teaching
Pedology	science of soils
Pelology	science of mud
Penology	science of crime and Punishment
Periodontics	science of gums
Peristerophily	science of collecting Pigeons
Pestology	science of pests
Petrology	science of rocks
Pharmacognosy	science of drugs of animal and plant origin
Pharmacology	science of drugs
Pharology	science of lighthouses
Pharyngology	science of throat
Phenology	science of organisms that are affected by climate

Phenomenology	science of phenomena
Philematology	science of kissing
Phillumeny	science of collecting matchbox labels
Philology	science of studying ancient texts; historical linguistics
Philosophy	science of knowledge and wisdom
Phoniatrics	science of studying and correcting speech defects
Phonology	science of speech sounds
Photobiology	science of studying the effects of light on organisms
Photonics	science of photons
Phraseology	science of phrases
Phrenology	science of studying bumps on the head
Phycology	science of algae and Seaweeds
Physics	science of matter and Energy
Physiology	science of studying the functions of each part of the body

Phytology	science of plants; botany
Piscatology	science of fishes
Pisteology	science of faith
Planetology	science of planets
Plumology	science of feathers
Plutology	science of political economy and wealth
Pneumatics	science of the mechanism of gases
Pneumonology	science of the diseases of the respiratory tract
Podiatry	science of studying the treatment of the disorders of the foot
Podology	science of the feet
Polemology	science of war
Pomology	science studying fruit growing plants
Pogonology	science of beards
Posology	science of quantity or Dosage
Potamology	science of rivers

Praxeology	science of efficient activity or action
Primatology	science of primates
Proctology	science of rectum, anus, and colon
Prosody	science of versification
Protistology	science of protists
Proxemics	science of studying man's need for personal space
Psalligraphy	science of paper–cutting to make pictures
Pseudology	science of lying
Pseudoptics	science of optical illusions
Psychobiology	science of studying the biology of the mind
Psychogenetics	science of internal and external mental states
Psychognosy	science of mentality, personality, and character
Psychology	science of human behavior
Psychopathology	science of mental illness
Psychophysics	science of studying the link between mental and physical processes

Pteridology science of ferns

Pterylology science of distribution of feathers on birds

Punnology science of puns

Pyretology science of fevers

Pyrgonology science of towers

Pyroballogy science of artillery

Pyrography science of wood-burning

Pyrotechnics science of combustion through fire or explosions

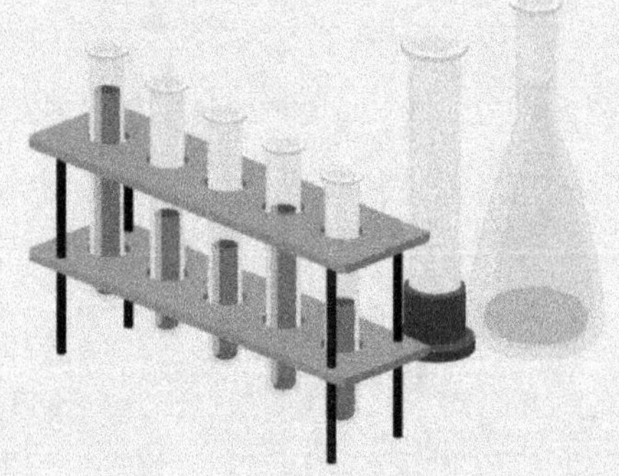

Quinology	science of quinine
Quantum computing	science of emerging technology that uses quantum mechanics to solve problems that cannot be solved by classical computers
Quantum mechanics	science that describes nature at the smallest scales of energy levels of atoms and subatomic particles
Queer theory	science of studying the issues related to sexual orientation and gender identity

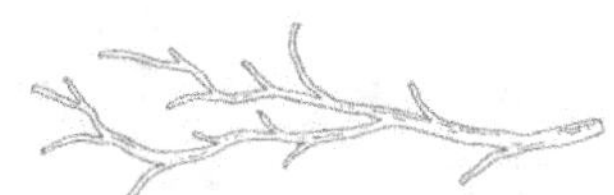

Raciology   science of studying racial differences

Radiobiology   science of studying the effects of the interaction of ionizing radiation with living matter

Radiochemistry   science of studying the ordinary chemical reactions under radioactive circumstances

Radiology   science of x – rays and their medical applications

Reflexology   science of reflexes

Rheology   science of deformation or flow of matter

Rheumatology   science of rheumatism

Rhochrematics   science of inventory management and the movement of products

Runology   science of runes

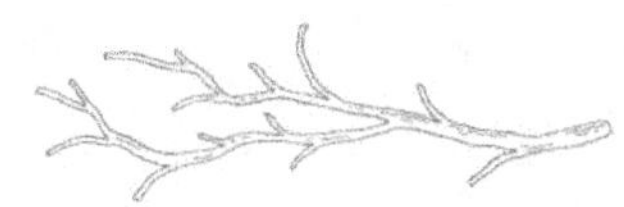

Sarcology	science of fleshy parts of the body
Satanology	science of studying the devil
Scatology	science of excrement or obscene literature
Schematonics	science of using gestures to express tones
Sciagraphy	science of shading
Scripophily	science of collecting bonds and share certificates
Sedimentology	science of sediments
Seismology	science of earthquakes
Selenodesy	science of shapes and features of the moon
Selenology	science of the moon
Semantics	science of meanings
Semantology	science of the meaning of words
Semasiology	science of meanings; semantics
Semiology	science of signs and signals
Semiotics	science of signs and symbols

Serology	science of serum
Sexology	science of sexual behavior
Siderology	science of iron and alloys' including steel
Significs	science of meaning
Silvics	science of studying tree's life
Sindonology	science of shroud of Turin
Sinology	science of studying China
Sitology	science of dietetics
Sociobiology	science of studying the biological basis of human behavior
Sociology	science of society
Solid mechanics	science of studying the behavior of solid materials
Somatology	science of substances
Sophiology	science of ideas
Soteriology	science of theological salvation
Snow hydrology	science of snow
Spectrology	science of ghosts

Spectroscopy	science of the spectra
Speleology	science of exploring the caves
Spermology	science of seeds
Sphagnology	science of peat moss
Sphygmology	science of pulse
Splanchnology	science of viscera
Spongology	science of sponges
Stasiology	science of political parties
Statics	science of bodies and forces in equilibrium
Stellar Astronomy	science of stars, their origin, and evolution
Stemmatology	science of studying the relationship between text
Stereochemistry	science of studying the relative spatial arrangement of atoms that form the structure of molecules and their manipulation
Stoichiology	science of elements and animal tissues
Stomatology	science of mouth

Storiology	science of folk tales
Stratigraphy	science of geological layers or strata
Stratography	science of leading an army
Stylometry	science of studying literature by means of statistical analysis
Suicidology	science of suicide
Supramolecular chemistry	science of studying the chemistry of assembled molecular sub–units
Symbology	science of symbols
Symptomatology	science of symptoms of illness
Synecology	science of ecological communities
Synectics	science of processes of invention
Syntax	science of sentence structure
Syphilology	science of syphilis

Systematics

science of the diversification of living forms, both past and present

Systematology

science of systems

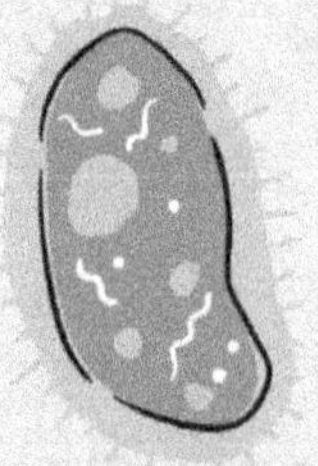

Taxidermy	science of curing and stuffing animals
Taxonomy	science of identifying, classifying, and naming organisms
Tectonics	science of the structure of objects, buildings, and landforms
Tegestology	science of collecting beer mats
Teleology	science of studying final causes, analysis in terms of purpose
Telmatology	science of swamps
Tempestology	science of tropical cyclones
Teratology	science of studying birth defects and later abnormalities in living organisms
Terrestrial Ecology	science of the terrestrial environment
Teuthology	science of cephalopods
Textology	science of production of texts
Thalassography	science of the sea

Thanatology	science of death and its customs
Thaumatology	science of miracles
Theoretical computer science	science of combining computers science and mathematics
Theriogenology	science of studying animals' reproductive systems
Thermodynamics	science of studying the relationship of heat to motion
Thermokinematics	science of the motion of heat
Thermology	science of heat
Therology	science of wild animals
Thremmatology	science of breeding domestic animals and plants
Threpsology	science of nutrition
Todilogy	science of tides
Timbrology	science of postage stamps
Tocology	science of obstetrics; midwifery
Tokology	science of childbirth

Tonetics	science of pronunciation
Topography	science of studying the shape and features of the land surface
Topology	science of studying places and their natural features
Toponymics	science of studying place – names
Toreutics	science of artistic works in metal
Toxicology	science of poisons
Toxophily	science of archery
Traumatology	science of wounds and their effects
Tribology	science of friction and wear between surfaces
Trichology	science of hair and its disorders
Trophology	science of nutrition
Tsiganology	science of gypsies
Turbology	science of tornadoes
Turnery	science of turning in a lathe

Typhlology	science of blindness and the blind
Typography	science of printing or using type
Typology	science of studying the types of things

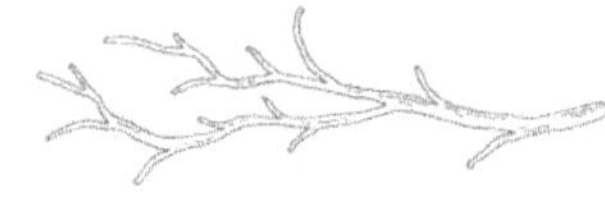

Uranography	science of descriptive astronomy and mapping
Uranology	science of studying the heavens; astronomy
Urbanology	science of studying cities
Urenology	science of rust molds
Urology	science of studying urine and the urinary tract

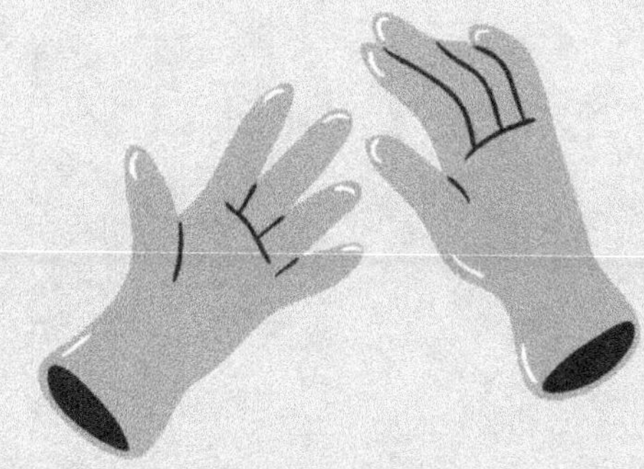

Venereology	science of venereal disease
Veterinary medicine	science of studying domesticated animals
Vexillology	science of flags
Victimology	science of studying victims
Vinology	science of studying wines and winemaking
Virology	science of viruses
Vitrics	science of glassy materials; glassware
Volcanology	science of volcanoes

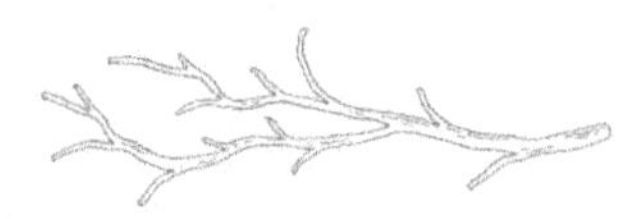

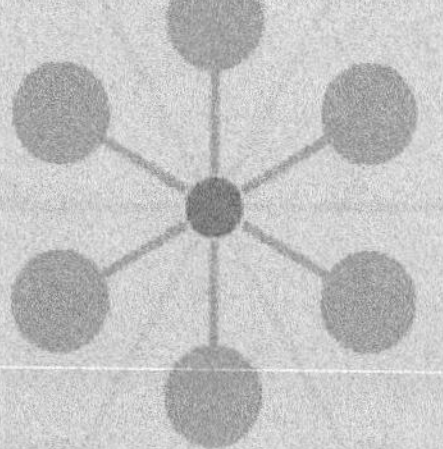

Xenobiology   science of biological
                              systems which do not exist
                              in nature

Xylography   science of engraving on
                              wood

Xylology   science of wood

Zenography science of studying the planet Jupiter

Zooarcheology science of studying animal remains of archeological sites

Zoochemistry science of the chemistry of animals

Zoogepgraphy science of geographic distribution of animals

Zoogeology science of fossil animal remains

Zoology science of animals

Zoonomy science of animal physiology

Zoonosology science of animal diseases

Zoopathology science of animal diseases

Zoophysics science of animal bodies

Zoophysiology science of the physiology of animals

Zoophytology science of plant-like animals

Zoosemiotics science of animal communication

REFERENCES:

Merriam Webster (https;//www.merriam –
webster.com/dictionary/arc
helogy)
"Eidology" (https://www.thefreedictionary.com/eidology)

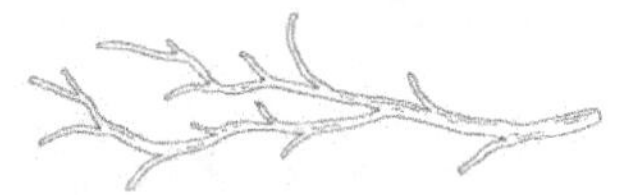

ABOUT THE AUTHOR

Roy B. Basa, LPT, PhD, DHum, DMin, DSc, FRIEdr

Roy Basa was born and raised in Murcia, Negros Occidental, Philippines by Raul and Lilia Basa together with his other 6 siblings. He graduated his elementary education from Lopez Jaena Elementary School. He then went to La Consolacion College, Murcia for his secondary education where he graduated as Class Valedictorian of 1998. He got his Bachelor's in Education major in General Science, Masters in School Administration and Supervision, and Doctor of Philosophy major in Educational Management at University of Negros Occidental – Recoletos where he graduated with Outstanding in Dissertation and High Academic Excellence Awards. He then took another masterate, the Master in Natural Science at University of St. La Salle, Bacolod under a scholarship grant, Project – Free Paglaum.

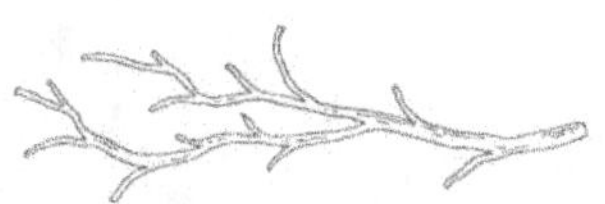